This Is How You Do It, Kid…

The *Inventor*preneur's Handbook

Francisco Guerra

For Frankie

CONTENTS

ACKNOWLEDGMENTS

Of all the words that have been strung together for this book, none of them are as difficult as these. Gratitude is more easily expressed than written, and there's always the fear of leaving someone out, of unintentionally slighting someone. (If that ends up being you, I apologize now.) But because no man's journey is without the aid of another's, then let me take a moment to thank a few key people who have been mentors, encouragers, teachers, inspirations and, last but certainly not least, friends.

The late Michael Picora, who first introduced me to the concept of licensing and who graciously shared his knowledge and friendship. I miss you, my friend.

To Brian and Angie Glover, who have been with me through every step of this process. We've made some pretty incredible things together.

Thanks also to the South Florida Inventor's Club—where I first found my "people"—motivational wonder Tony Robbins whose unerring ability to inspire others has helped propel me forward along this path to success.

To David Barman, a dear friend and ally, and to the countless other executives who I've had the pleasure of watching and emulating their leadership style.

And, of course, a particular thanks to my uncommonly insightful friend, NYT Bestselling author Rhonda Nelson, whose assistance in the writing of this book has been invaluable and greatly appreciated.

Francisco Guerra

INTRODUCTION

It's the million-dollar question—*how did you do it?*

How did you take your mere idea from invention to fruition, from a what-if to a done-deal? An *aha!* moment to a ballooning bank account and properties all over the world? Did you come from a wealthy family? Attend the best colleges and business schools in the country? Learn the infamous secret handshake? Find the silver bullet?

The answer to those first three questions I'll outline in the book, but the answer to last few is a laughable, resounding no. *No, no, no.* Born in Cuba, my strictly working-class family arrived in Miami when I was five-years-old and, while I've since obtained a variety of degrees from institutions and colleges all over the country, when I patented my first successful invention, the only master's I could claim with any confidence had been courtesy of the proverbial School of Hard-knocks. (And it's still my most treasured alma mater.)

When it comes to being a profitable inventor, there is no secret handshake or magical silver bullet. There's merely a mechanism to success and once you've learned how to work the mechanism, to be both an inventor and an entrepreneur—an *inventor*preneur, if you will—then the process becomes quite simple.

It only *appears* complicated.

You'll notice that I've dedicated this book to my son, Frankie, and he's ultimately the reason I've chosen to write it.

In the following pages, I'm going to tell you what I wish someone had told me when I first began this journey more than twenty years ago. It's my fondest wish that my hindsight will be his—and your—20/20, because I would have loved for someone to affectionately grab me by the scruff of the neck and say, "*Listen up and pay attention. This is how you do it, kid…*"

STEP ONE: FINDING YOUR PASSION

"Passion is the genesis of genius." —Anthony Robbins

Sounds too simple, right? Find your passion. Figure out what it is that you love to do and then figure out a way to make a living doing it.

Yeah, yeah, I know. This isn't new advice. You've undoubtedly heard it before, from people with a lot of alphabet listed after the name on their door or letterhead. But the reason you've heard it before—the reason that this little nugget of insight turns up more often than any other—is because it's *significant*. It's *key*. It's *necessary*.

Because passion is the catalyst.

It's what ignites the flame of ambition, sets blaze to purpose, incinerates doubt and turns a deaf ear to naysayers. Passion fuels the pursuit of knowledge, the courage to dream a bigger dream. It doesn't hear "no," it continually refreshes the flagging will with the whisper of "you can do it" and "what if?" and "try again" and "just maybe…"

Much like Superman's ability to fly or Wonder Woman's Lasso of Truth, passion is the undisputed super power of the successful. It's that secret little something that inspires faith and refuses to quit. In a world which is increasingly rewarding mediocrity, it's the lone rustler cutting the trophy winners away from the ever-growing herd of participation ribbon people.

Don't think you're smart enough to do what you want to do? Educated enough? Don't think you have the resources to make your dream happen? That you have the right connections? That you've got what it takes?

Guess what? *You're wrong.* Passion will level the playing field.

Listen, passion doesn't care if you didn't graduate from high school, if years of standardized testing placed you right smack in the middle of the "of average intelligence" group. It doesn't care who your parents were, where they came from or how much money was in their bank account. It's the ultimate equalizer, because if you're passionate about whatever it is that you want to do or make happen, then none of those things will matter.

You will succeed because passion won't let you fail.

Whether it's an invention you want to take to market, a service you want to provide, even a lowly idea with grand aspirations, passion will inspire you to learn *absolutely* everything you can about what's captured your attention and set your imagination on fire. That knowledge will give you the confidence to boldly pick up the phone and knock on doors. That confidence will help you cultivate those connections.

You see, passion detonates interest, interest creates knowledge, knowledge inspires confidence and that chain reaction culminates with—*tada!*—a result. And that's the goal, right? (If it's not, then you need to go back to the drawing board.)

To illustrate my point, I'm going to tell you a story. In my early twenties I was a magician on a cruise ship. I'd gotten into magic in my late teens as a direct result of some sibling rivalry between me and my younger brother. He was a natural juggler, seriously talented and, while I had passable skill (translation: not as good) I found that I could master a magic trick in less time and get a better response from an audience.

Economics at its finest and my first *aha!* moment, one that would ultimately chart a course that would change my life forever.

You see, magic was *my* passion.

Finding something that intrigued and excited me—that I knew to the very marrow of my bones that I was good at—absolutely set my life ablaze. It grabbed me by the throat and wouldn't let go. It didn't matter that friends and loved ones thought I was wasting my time, that I was squandering my life "playing" instead of working at a "real" job. The only thing that mattered was getting better, learning more, honing my craft.

I didn't want to just be good, or good enough—I wanted to be the best.

Thanks to that enthusiasm and tenacity, it wasn't long until I was hosting my own shows, selling tricks and illusions—some of them for thousands of dollars—to other magicians, and I ultimately landed a much-coveted job as a spokesperson for Nabisco, traveling all over the US. (There's another story there, which I will get to later, but for now back to the cruise ship.)

This particular cruise line toured the southern Caribbean and once every two weeks dropped anchor in Puerto Rico. A fellow magician and friend routinely disembarked there and would do a show for the local children's hospital, and finally harassed and harangued me enough that I agreed to do it with him.

I'll be honest—I didn't want to. I dreaded it. I can't even tell you why. Call it fatigue, call it laziness, call it whatever… The idea of facing those sick children struck a sympathetic note in my chest that I'd just as soon avoid.

It was with that admittedly poor attitude that I reluctantly followed my friend into the building. It was a serviceable concrete block structure—in other words "cheap"—with dingy white walls and old pale green tile, the kind that had covered almost every school cafeteria I'd ever visited. It smelled like antiseptic and sweat—sanitized poverty. It was claustrophobic, depressing, a sense of hopelessness permeating the very air. The nuns led us down a long, low-ceilinged hall and my anxiety climbed with each step deeper into the building.

I couldn't believe I'd let myself get roped into this. I could have stayed on the ship, gotten some much-needed rest. I could have worked on my act. I could have flirted with Sheila, the new blackjack dealer. The truth was, I would have rather been anywhere at that moment than there, in that sad little hospital in Puerto Rico.

And then I walked into the multipurpose room and everything changed.

Hundreds of children, all of them wearing an identical expression of expectation, of excitement. Even the older ones, who thought they were too cool for this sort of thing. Ask any performer what makes a show and they'll tell you that it's the audience, period. It's action and reaction, the trick and the response, the illusion and the startled gasp or the breathless "ahhhh!" The energy in this particular audience was palpable, made my skin prickle, my heart race.

It was then that I saw him, his expression more expectant, more eager than any other. His face pressed against the glass of a small room built into the back wall, he watched the entire act from start to finish, in utter, fixated, *rapt* attention.

He was in isolation from the other children—leukemia, I would later find out—and his name was Carlos.

Because he'd enjoyed the show so much, more than anyone else in the room, I decided to give him a private performance. I spent thirty minutes with the kid, gave him all of my best stuff, even some things I was still working on, and he loved every single minute of it.

Loved it.

Magic, I discovered, was his passion, too.

Carlos made me promise to come back and I assured him that I would. What I'd imagined was going to be a horrible experience had turned into one of the most professionally and personally rewarding I'd ever had in my life.

"What do you want me to do next time?" I asked him as I was packing up to leave. "What would you like to see?"

I'll never forget the expression on his face. He smiled, almost wistfully, and looked and me and said, "I want to see it snow."

Snow? Really? Right. Didn't see that one coming. At the time I didn't have any idea how on earth I was going to make it snow in a tropical climate, much less in a cramped little hospital room for a terminally ill child, but I knew that I had to make it happen because I'd said I would.

For the next two weeks every free minute I had was devoted to developing a device that would replicate snow. I'd always had a knack for using household items in nontraditional ways to aid in my illusions—I'd once used rolling window shades mounted to the inside of a large box to make myself "appear" in what had been a seemingly empty space—so I knew that there had to be a way to do it.

Lots of trial and error, lots of frustrated grumbling and swearing under my breath, but by the end of the second week, I'd done it. I'd packed the device into an old doctor's bag and the minute we pulled into port, I was off the boat and on my way to the hospital. I knew that I'd made something special and I couldn't wait to share it with the kid who'd inspired it. I hurried down the hall, through the double doors into the multipurpose area, toward Carlos's isolation room…only to discover that it was empty.

He'd lost his battle with cancer three days before I'd arrived.

It breaks my heart that the boy I'd originally designed my very first snow machine for—the Snowman™— never got to see it, but because of him and his simple, seemingly odd request, literally *millions* of people all over the world have experienced the magic of that machine. It's in every major theme park in the world—Disneyworld, Disneyland, Universal Studios, SeaWorld, Busch Gardens. It's been used in countless films—Harry Potter, Twilight, Elf, The Grinch, just to name a few—as well as videos for megastars Taylor

Swift, Miranda Lambert and Justin Bieber.

It was my break-out invention, the one that ultimately launched my career as a serial inventor and has put me at the helm of the largest special effects company in the world.

It was the game-changer, my friends, and if I can do it, then you can too.

STEP TWO: IDENTIFYING THE MARKET—
WHO WANTS WHAT YOU HAVE?

"The aim of marketing is to know and understand your customer so well the product and service fits him and sells itself."—Peter Drucker

So you've found your passion and you've learned everything you possibly can about it. You're pumped up, you're psyched, you're ready to take the world by storm.

Excellent, chief, because you're going to need that energy.

For market research.

Sorry for knocking the wind out of your sails, but it's the truth. It doesn't matter how excited you are about your idea if there isn't a marketable need for it. If no one is interested in what you have, then this is a *large* obstacle. One that can more than likely be surmounted with a little re-envisioning and initiative, but it's still a potential problem.

Let me give you an example. Once upon a time, when Frankie was a toddler, he loved the indoor playgrounds featured at many of the fast-food restaurants. He especially loved the ball pits. So I'm sitting there watching him one day, and a nearby kid loses his diaper and proceeds to mark his immediate territory. (A very different kind of golden arch, let me tell you.) Another kid has long ropes of snot hanging from his nose, and another is cramming one of the balls into his mouth.

Ew.

It's a germ-infested, unsanitary mess and, because I'm an inventor and inventors admittedly think differently from the rest of the world, my brain immediately starts looking for a solution to clean those balls. Days later I'd produced my first prototype. It was a device that vacuumed the balls from the pit, spun them through a cleaning/sanitizing solution, then dried them and shot the balls into an awaiting container. Brilliant, yes? I thought so. So much so, in fact, that I sunk a large chunk of capital into the idea and Fran's Lickety-Split Ball-Cleaning business was born.

And subsequently died a swift, costly death…because I failed to do the necessary market research. I just assumed that every fast food restaurant on the planet with those nasty ball-pits would want my services.

I assumed wrong.

Those businesses are primarily franchised out to individual owners who would rather pay a minimum-wage employee to do the job with a garden hose than hire a professional outside source. Unsurprisingly, this would have been helpful to know *before* I went to the time, trouble and expense to invent, design, and manufacture a machine to do the job, then open and staff a start-up to handle what I imagined would become a multi-million dollar business.

Hindsight, remember?

Do your homework. Research your market. And just when you think you've done all the research you can do, go back and do it again. Trust me on this.

Had I taken the time to actually go in and speak to a few of those restaurant owners and managers and said, "Look, this is what I've got, isn't this fantastic, would you be interested in hiring Fran's Lickety-Split Ball-Cleaning Business to remove the urine and snot and spilled coke and French fry crumbs from your ball pit?" and actually *listened* to their response, I'd have avoided this rookie mistake.

That said, don't be afraid to think big. Don't be afraid to explore alternate uses for whatever it is that you have. Did you know that Play-Doh's original purpose was to clean coal and soot from the walls of people's homes? It's true. When cleaner energy sources became available and sales nose-dived, the original company faced bankruptcy. It wasn't until one of the owner's noticed that his sister, who was a school teacher, was allowing her students to use it as molding clay, that the "toy" purpose was discovered. They added a scent—to cover up the old, less appealing one—and rebranded. That's ingenuity.

People, as a rule, tend to overcomplicate things, particularly when they're dealing with the unknown, and that's especially true when it comes to the accidental inventor. We've all heard the old saying, "Necessity is the mother of invention" and I can't imagine that truer words have ever been spoken. From the 1930's housewife who complained to her husband that she needed something to hold her fashionable "bob cut" in place—thus the bobby pin—to the Kellogg brothers who were looking for healthier eating choices for their patients and inadvertently stumbled upon Corn Flakes, need has driven the market.

Need will *always* drive the market.

Say you've invented something similar to an existing product already on the shelves, or a service that's already being provided, but your product or service is different. (And, one would hope, better.) How do you find out if there's room in the market for your idea?

First order of business—look at who's already manufacturing and distributing what's out there.

When I made the decision to take my first snow machine to market, I went into every big box store in my area and combed through their Christmas and party sections. I looked at every product that was even remotely similar to mine—or served the same sort of purpose—and, using my trusty recorder, I collected the names of the manufacturers and the distributors. It wasn't hard. The information was *right there.* Oftentimes, even the address.

Armed with that information, I came home, thoroughly researched the various companies and put together cut sheets—an overview with spec details—and mailed (yes, mailed them, the good old-fashioned way) to each potential client, asking if they'd be interested in licensing my product.

Within four days of those packets going out, I had an offer of $50,000 in advance against royalties.

So what was the difference between the ball-cleaning business and the snow machine? *Demand.* A bigger market.

Much bigger, it would turn out, than I'd ever dreamed.

You see, after Carlos passed away, I brought the snow machine back and put it up on a shelf, where it subsequently sat for two years. I'd custom-made the illusion for him and had been reluctant to share it with anyone else. It wasn't until the City Manager of Hialeah , Florida came to see me about borrowing some things from me for their company picnic that it ultimately resurfaced.

I'll never forget it. We were out in my shop, looking through my carefully labeled inventory, picking out various items for Robbie to use at the picnic when suddenly his gaze landed on the machine.

"Snow machine?" he asked, a brow lifting in surprise. Remember, we're in my shop. There's everything from a guillotine to a high wire set-up in there and the snow machine is what catches his attention? *Really?*

"Oh, yeah," I said, immediately thinking of Carlos. "It's actually kind of neat. Here, let me show you."

So I pulled the machine down from the shelf, loaded the solution and then powered it up. Thousands of realistic-looking flakes suddenly floated in the air. It's a hundred degrees outside and I've just made it snow. Even I was impressed.

So was Robbie.

He smiled and shot me a speculative look. "Can you build more of these? Make them bigger?"

I nodded. "Sure."

"Excellent. I want to use them for the Christmas Tree lighting."

As promised, I built the machines and they worked beautifully. Even better than I'd ever imagined.

Strategically positioned around an area of Goodlet Park, a balmy 54 degrees, when my snow started drifting slowly from the night sky, backlit from the holiday lights and silhouetted against the palm trees, a delighted hush moved through the crowd and literally transformed the event. In the space of a heartbeat it went from amazing to *awesome*, from an occasion to genuine *entertainment*.

There's something magical, almost romantic and definitely nostalgic about snow. From Bing Crosby's *White Christmas*, to *Frosty the Snowman*, to those keenly anticipated Snow Days school children hope for. For some inexplicable reason, snow has the unique power to bring out the kid in all of us—and, as I looked at the smiling, awe-struck expressions of the crowd gathered there in the park that night, I felt it all the way down to my little toes.

As it happened, there was a Disney executive from the film division in attendance as well and, to my eternal thankfulness, he felt it too.

Hello, Hollywood.

Francisco Guerra

STEP THREE: SECURE THE INTELLECTUAL PROPERTY—PROTECT YOUR PASSION

The Congress shall have the Power... To promote the Progress of Science and useful Arts, be securing for limited Times to Authors and Inventors the Exclusive right to their respective Writings and Discoveries." –The US Constitution; Article I, Section 8

At the height of my career as a magician I was making a million bucks a year. Fantastic, right? Yes...but I was also *spending* a million bucks a year and, after watching an eighty-year-old man still pulling a rabbit out of his hat, I knew that I needed to figure out another way to build wealth. Don't get me wrong—I *loved* what I was doing, was as happy as I could be—but I knew that my current pace wasn't sustainable, that eventually I wouldn't be able to work as hard as I was working at the time, and I thought, man, there has to be an easier way. I wanted to do something that would make money while I slept.

At the time I was inventing illusions and selling them to other magicians, but my audience was limited to five-thousand. I knew that if I was ever going to build the fortune I wanted I would need to widen the scope, cast a broader net.

With that goal in mind, I took a four month sabbatical and I asked myself, what do the wealthiest people in the world do? How did they amass their fortunes? So I started researching and studying, and I realized that they all had one thing in common—they owned patents, copyrights, trademarks or trade secrets. Once I knew what each one of those things were and how they worked—once I realized that *all* of those things were in my everyday life—I knew that I'd found the ultimate source to achieve my goals. All I had to do was tap into it.

So what was I going to tap into *exactly?*

Intellectual Property.

No doubt it's the biggest stumbling block of the budding inventor, but don't worry. I'm going to give you the benefit of my twenty-plus years' experience dealing with this process and, hopefully, prevent you from making any lengthy, costly mistakes.

Let's begin with the basics, shall we? Dictionary.com describes intellectual property as follows: (noun) *Law.* property that results from original creative thought, as patents, copyright material and trademarks.

It's that simple little word "property" that ultimately separates an idea from an invention.

I know, I know, it's one of those things that invariably makes the person on the other side of my desk cock their head in baffled confusion, a look that strongly reminds me of Scooby Doo.

"But Francisco, that can't be right!" they'll protest. "How can I possibly not own the very thoughts in my head? An idea borne of my very own imagination? It's *my* idea."

I hate to break it to you, kid, but an idea is utterly useless unless you do something with it.

Sounds harsh, doesn't it? Sorry, but it's the truth. What if Thomas Edison had only ever had the *idea* for the first commercially practical light bulb, or the phonograph, or the two-way telegraph system? What if Henry Ford had only had the *idea* for assembly-line manufacturing? Eli Whitney the cotton gin? I could go on and on, but you get the idea, I'm sure.

Absolutely *everything* around you is an invention.

I want you to do a quick inventory of your surroundings and think about that for a moment. *Everything.* From your favorite comfortable chair, to the television you watch, to the book or eReader you're holding in your hand right now, right down to the technology it took to make those things work.

It's *all* an invention.

Wow. Profound, isn't it?

Someone somewhere at *some* point in time thought of it, then took it one step further and *created* it. *That's* the difference.

Let me give you an example. Say a guy makes an appointment with my licensing firm, walks into my office—much to my amusement they usually eye the electric chair sitting in the corner first—then he takes a seat and very excitedly says, "Guess what, Fran? I've got an invention."

"You do? Brilliant. Tell me about it." The eternal optimist, I lean forward, waiting to be blown away.

A deep breath, then, "I want to host expeditions to the moon, be the Indiana Jones of outer space. I've even got a name for my spaceship—'Moon Raider.'"

Oh, boy. Admittedly, I'm blown away, but not in the way I'd hoped. "I hate to be the bearer of bad news, but that's an idea, not an invention."

Cue the Scooby Doo look. "What do you mean it's not an invention? I checked the internet first. Listen," he tells me, as though he's imparting a juicy secret. "No one is hosting expeditions to the moon, and the domain name for Moon Raider is *wide* open."

Imagine that.

"I'm about to pull the trigger on that little piece of web space."

Fantastic. That'll be the worst $5.95 he'll ever spend. Unfortunately, I see this kind of thing all the time. I'd say roughly three-quarters of the people who come through my door have ideas, but not actual inventions. "Let me ask you something. Do you have a spaceship?"

"Er…no." Evidently this was a detail that, in his excitement, he overlooked.

"Then how are you going to get to the moon?"

He gives a me a blank look, one that still holds an unfortunate amount of optimism. "I'm not sure. Should we talk to NASA?"

Er, no.

The next day another gentleman shows up. He, too, wants to go to the moon, but this guy has actually drafted a *design* of a spaceship. His drawings are impressive, he's done his homework, and validated the technology.

He has an actual invention. Ah, now we're cookin', aren't we? And because he has an actual invention, first order of business—protect it.

Even as early as ancient Greece, man has understood the value of guarding the creations of the mind, whether it's an invention or a work of art. For instance, in the city of Sybaris—which was destroyed in 510 BC—leaders decreed:

"If a cook invents a delicious new dish, no other cook is permitted to prepare that dish for one year. During that time, only the inventor can reap the commercial profits from his dish. This will motivate others to work hard and compete in such inventions."

Look at that—they protected and rewarded the inventor, and encouraged innovation all in one fell swoop. The key components of commerce all wrapped up in a neat little package. Brilliant, right?

When I began to understand the value of Intellectual Property—the beach front real estate of global business—and patents, in particular, I went through my inventory of good ideas and knew that I had two. The first I'd unwittingly undersold when I was twenty, and the technology later emerged on the market as a popular floor cleaning device. It's a little thing called the Swiffer. You might have heard of it.

The second was my snow machine.

My first official patent, it stopped competitors from making and selling knock-offs of my design, and kicked off what would ultimately be my intellectual property career. When my patent finally came through, and I held it in my hands and read the first line—"Guerra is the first to..."

Oh, man. *Absolutely amazing.* The *first* to. Not the second or the third or any other number. The *first*. A trophy moment. Powerful stuff, I'll tell you.

Fantastic, Fran. But how did you do it?

Listen, here's the deal. I'm not going to give you all the technical terms and conditions of Intellectual Property. There have been countless books written by people much more qualified than myself who have done that, and that information is readily available with a quick Google search. Heck, uspto.gov gives instructions on how to properly file a patent. That information is cheap, it's out there. It's easily found for the motivated and, as an *inventor*preneur, it's your job make use of the resources available and educate yourself.

No, the purpose of this book—what I want Frankie to know—is how *I* did it, how I streamlined the system into a machine that works for me and every client who comes through my door.

When I was finally ready to file the first patent, I went and bought a book, complete with tear-out worksheets, and I read it from cover to cover several times—See? Available resources and education—and then I met with an attorney. In speaking with him, I noticed that he asked lots of questions and took even more notes, that he seemed to know less about it, frankly, than I did, and I'd come seeking his very expensive advice. It wasn't until he slipped up and mentioned his "patent agent" I realized that he was outsourcing the work. Did you hear that?

Another *aha!* moment.

Rather than pay the attorney to get the information I needed, I decided to cut out the middle man and work directly with the supplier—the patent agent—and that's the *Absolute Best* advice I can give you.

Don't try to do it yourself. There are too many things that can go wrong—too many variables in play—and, in all probability, you'll end up losing rights you should have kept. Throughout this book I've encouraged you to do your due diligence, to research and educate yourself and that still applies—it will *always* apply.

There is no lazy way to succeed.

But there's a time to take initiative and there's a time to admit you're potentially out of your depth. This is one of them.

Delegate to a professional in the field. Contact either a patent agent or a patent attorney. Let them fill out and file the paperwork. Trust me on this. It's their job to know the law, the procedure, the rules and regulations, and your time is much better spent elsewhere. Like working on other inventions and pursuing licensing agreements for products already in the patent pipeline.

I actually filed my first patent myself—didn't do too bad a job of it, I'm proud to say—but when my first office action arrived (the patent office's polite way of saying "Sorry, pal, try again") I handed everything over to a patent agent and let him see it forward from there.

Best decision I ever made.

Good friend and Patent Attorney David Barman and I have been working together for more than twenty years, and he's been no small part of my success. An agent when we started, I put him through law school and ultimately helped him open his own practice.

Second Best advice I can give you, son? Invest in good people. They're worth it.

STEP FOUR: PREPARE YOUR PRESENTATION—IT'S SHOWTIME!

"Forewarned, forearmed; to be prepared is half the victory."—Miguel de Cervantes

Undoubtedly, this step is one of the most intimidating, particularly if you're an inexperienced public speaker or struggle with being the center of attention. You know what makes it easier?

Practice.

Rehearse, rehearse, rehearse. Know your information backward and forward. Present to friends until you're comfortable with every aspect of your pitch, until it feels utterly and completely natural.

In addition to your working prototype, which we will get to shortly, put together an executive summary. This short essay will give you key talking points and help keep you on track when your tongue starts to get too big for your mouth or your hands begin to sweat. Additionally, it will keep your audience engaged in what you're selling—key thing, there—and will prevent them from answering texts or playing games on their phones. The instant you hear the tell-tale sounds of Candy Crush you can forget it, chief. You've lost them.

Game over. Opportunity wasted.

You've only got one shot at making a good impression

and if you blow it… It's onto the next meeting or learning how to say, "Do you want fries with that?" No pressure, right? Wrong. And that's a good thing. Because pressure is what's going to make sure that you're as prepared as you can be. Pressure will ensure that you've dotted all your I's and crossed all you're T's. Pressure will urge you to check and recheck your working prototype.

Ah, the working prototype—the single-most important tool in the arsenal of your presentation. Ultimately, nothing else you're going to say is going to matter if you're unable to communicate the purpose of your invention, and nothing is going to showcase it better than visible proof of its function.

Let me give you an example. Awhile back I had a client come through the door who'd been issued a design patent on half of a duck butt. Yes, you read that right.

Half of a duck butt.

This gentleman owned a hunting company and sold hunting supplies and novelties. A large portion of his business was generated through avid duck hunters. When he tossed his prototype onto my desk, I'll admit that initially I was a bit skeptical and slightly repulsed. On one side were the pretty duck feathers, the other three large suction cups. It was designed to stick to the windshield of a car or truck, so that it looked like the duck had been struck by the vehicle and had launched through the glass. Not anything I'm keen to affix to any of my own cars, I can tell you, but I'm not a duck hunter, so…

At any rate, when we landed our first presentation, the buyer we were targeting was just as mystified as I had been…until I walked around her desk and stuck it to her computer monitor.

Boom. Done. She got it.

Would she have been able to get it via a blue print or drawing? It's possible, but probably not. That visual gave it the wow-factor, and that's the goal. You want the buyer to look at the product, see its purpose or function and know exactly why they want it on their shelves.

Here's another example, this one with a less than stellar outcome.

Once upon a time in a land called China, me and my friend and current President of Global Home Retail, Peter Rocheleau, were pitching the snow machine to K-Mart. Big account, right? Very, very big deal. While Peter and I were in favor of going in and handling the presentation ourselves, another agent at K-Mart was certain she could do a better job and insisted on presenting on our behalf.

This was a mistake.

In the first place, the inventor inevitably becomes the master at whatever it is that he's invented. He becomes the specialist in the field. Why?

Because it's *his* invention.

Because it's *his* area of expertise.

Because he's taken it apart, put it back together, made improvements and modifications that have either not worked or have made it perform better. He knows the purpose of every nut and bolt, every gear, every bit of hardware from one end of the mechanism to the other.

Admittedly, the version of the snow machine that we were pitching that day wasn't at its best. There were two different switches, one that activated the solution and another that distributed the snow. When our overzealous representative went in and explained that, as a result of our machine, their customers would be able to not only produce snow for various occasions—birthday parties! bar mitzvahs! Anniversaries! and weddings!—as well as the Christmas season, but also "make it snow in July!" our initial hopes were pretty high.

Until she turned on the snow distributer…

And we watched in sickening horror as a giant blob of foamy, gelatinous snow shot across the boardroom table like an arrow to a bulls-eye and, to the tune of a collective startled gasp, landed right smack in the middle of the current President and CEO of K-Mart, Inc's chest. The sound it made as it found its target resonated like cannon fire in the eerily quiet room. Peter and I looked at each other, muttered a few choice words, then glanced back at the CEO, whose face had gone an alarming shade of red. The rep who'd inadvertently soiled and humiliated her boss shot us a death ray glare, then immediately launched into repair mode, but it was too late. The damage had been done.

She'd activated the solution a little too soon, which caused a build-up and, well... You know the rest of the story. Guess what? We didn't sell our snow machines in K-Mart and, in fact, have yet to sell *anything* to that company.

First impressions, kid. You only get one shot at it.

Which brings me to tip number two—be a professional. What do I mean by that? Let's start with the obvious. Dress the part. If you think it's cool to walk into a meeting in a pair of stained pants and a lab coat—the proverbial absentminded inventor—then you'd better think again, Jack. Suit and tie, matching socks, clean shoes. Privately you can be as eccentric as you want to be, but when it comes to conducting business in the corporate world, nobody wants to work with a nut. Prospective clients need to be able to trust you. Want to wave a big red flag at potential customers? Come in looking like you wandered off the set of *Honey, I Shrunk the Kids* and see how swiftly you're shown the door.

This is a no-brainer. Be a professional.

So what else does that mean, exactly? It means that you have to be a good communicator. It means that you've got to be able to get your message across in a way that engages the audience and convinces them a.) why your product needs to be on the market and b.) that you believe wholeheartedly in it.

Do you know what gets people excited? *Excitement.* It's infectious.

Don't be afraid to be in love with your invention. Don't be afraid to share your passion about it. That sort of enthusiasm is hard to fake and even harder to ignore. It gives you an instant connection with a potential client and once that connection is made, it's easier to get buy-in. And do you know what happens once you've got buy-in? You've got the client *invested* in your product to the point that it's not just your product—it's *theirs* too. That sense of ownership is critical because it creates a team mentality, a we're-in-this-together, how-can-we-make-this-better kind of environment that's the breeding ground of successful business relationships.

When pitching your product, be sure to explain how it's going to solve a problem, because the best inventions always do. For instance, Peter once developed a Christmas tree that sprang from the box and instantly bloomed into shape. What's the number one complaint from people who assemble and erect artificial trees? Putting them up, shaping the branches, making sure there are no unseemly holes in the foliage. It detracts from the fun part, which is hanging the ornaments, decorating the tree.

Peter's design eliminated that problem. Made from spring steel, for marketing purposes we renamed it "Memory Metal" and it sold like hotcakes. I actually invented a bubble wand that emerged from the bottle with a gentle squeeze, eliminating the need to dip your fingers into the solution and fish around for the instrument. When demonstrating I pretended like I'd lost the wand.

"Hmm. Where is it? I must have misplaced it…" I pretended to look for it, while I secretly gave the bottle a squeeze, making the wand lift past the solution.

"It's there," my potential buyer said, trying to be helpful.

"What?"

"There. In the bottle," she said with a nod.

I smiled, and her eyes widened. "*Ah.* Clever."

She got it. *Sold.*

See? It's not that difficult.

Here's the deal. These people *want* to see you. They *want* to see what you've got. They're all looking for the next big thing, the next *wow!* product that's going to give them an edge against their competitors. They're in the market of buying and you're in the market of selling. Use that to your advantage and don't be discouraged if the person you're pitching to doesn't get it. Sometimes they don't, but it doesn't mean they're right. Keep plugging away. When trying to get your foot in the door, be sure to utilize professional organizations like LinkedIn.com. Emails should be short and to the point, and should be devoid of links or trigger words that will land your correspondence in the spam filter. These people are busy. Don't waste their time with a long-winded message or hard sell when the purpose of the note is to secure a meeting. I receive literally *hundreds* of emails and text messages a day. *Hundreds.* Anything longer than a paragraph from an unknown person or a company that I don't recognize gets relegated to the bottom of the pile.

This is not the ideal place to be, trust me.

Here's another tip to keep in mind when attempting to garner that meeting. When conventional methods don't work, then consider sending the same message via a different source. I recently used this approach myself. A client contacted me and wanted me to get in touch with a former president of the United States on his behalf. This particular past president is super insulated, is *notoriously* difficult to reach, but where others had failed, I succeeded.

With a fax.

Ingenious, right? In an age where email and cell phones dominate the communication business, the humble, outdated fax machine did what those other methods couldn't. My fax was *hand delivered* into his office.

Mission accomplished.

Additional things to keep in mind when contacting various companies—ask first for the research and development department. If they don't have one, ask for engineering. If that doesn't work, move onto sales and marketing. If you strike out there, go directly to the top, to the CEO of the company. Frankly, I typically have more luck there than I do with any other department. Can you guess why?

Because that guy is like-minded—we're both entrepreneurs.

Here's something else to keep in mind. Always go into a

meeting with what we call a "hip-pocket" concession—something that you've already decided that you're willing to give up. Why? Because it demonstrates flexibility and makes the buyer feel like he's getting a little something extra in return. Everyone needs to feel like a winner.

In the event you aren't able to give the potential client a working prototype to have on hand after the initial meeting, then definitely be prepared with a leave-behind. A leave-behind? What's that? At the very least it's a business card with your contact information, but ideally a cut-sheet, detailing your product—an overview, cost to produce, potential markets, etc... You never want to walk away without giving the potential client tangible proof of your product and your contact information.

Back to preparation, have non-disclosure documents on-hand—you're a professional, remember?—but don't get upset if the client refuses to sign them. There's always the possibility that they're working on a similar design and signing your document would tie their hands. It's not in their professional interests, and it shouldn't be a deal breaker for you.

At the end of the day, you want to build a lasting relationship with these companies. You don't want to be a one-hit wonder. You want to add more and more to your inventory and, ultimately, into theirs. You're not just selling your product, you're selling yourself, and your future business. Remember, you want this relationship to last. You're not in it for a quick buck—you're in it for the long haul.

Be prepared. Be a professional and, above all, make it count, kid.

Francisco Guerra

STEP FIVE: BE STRATEGIC—FAKE IT 'TIL YOU MAKE IT

"All successful people have a goal. No one can get anywhere unless he knows where he wants to go."—Norman Vincent Peale

Back in the early days of my career, I owned a company called the Bombino Brothers Entertainment Troupe. I'd parlayed my experience and various props from my magic act into the entertainment business and catered to large corporate events—grand openings, company picnics, retirement dinners, etc...

In the beginning I played a lot of beat-the-check-to-the-bank, but knew that if I could just get the business off the ground that it would ultimately net a decent income. Part of that income, I knew, would come from repeat bookings from the bigger companies and their subsidiaries. And the gatekeepers to these companies and my future success?

The human resources managers.

So I'm a little fish in a big pond, right? But to land the business I needed to secure to grow into the formidable, profitable company I knew that we could become, I had to *front* like a big fish.

This concept occurs in nature all the time. Male peacocks

spread their feathers, gorillas straighten and beat their chests, the cobra flares its neck, the puffer fish inflates. Even men draw their shoulders back and flex a few muscles when trying to show themselves to their best advantage. Why?

To *appear* bigger. Because bigger is better, right?

While some might argue that letting your bulldog mouth overload your Chihuahua butt might be a potentially disastrous business practice, I've found that, for the most part, the risk is typically worth the reward.

Picture this. It's June, 1993. I'm a fit energetic twenty something with more confidence than experience, and enough initiative and intelligence to be slightly, shall we say...reckless. Hey, it is what it is, kid. Hindsight is a beautiful teacher and there's nothing more humbling than failure. I've had my fair share of that, believe me, and am as proud of those so-called failures as I am my successes. I learned something from each and every one, the most significant of which was the immeasurable value of trying again.

Anyone can fail and quit—it takes courage to try again— and since courage is the cornerstone of character, I look at each one of those losses as the building blocks of my integrity, the square of my principles, the yardstick of my sense of honor.

Anyway, back to 1993. Bombino Brothers is in the middle of a cash flow crisis and, though I'm a skilled magician, even I don't have the ability to make money magically appear in the bank account. At this point I've got a master's in "creative finance," creditors are ringing our phone off the hook—always one to look for the silver lining, I congratulated myself for having a phone they could *actually* call—and payroll is due. I've got a meeting with the head of a large entertainment company and, bottom line, I need this business.

I need it.

Landing this account would put us immediately in the black, would generate some much-needed income for months, but more importantly, would put Bombino Brothers on the radar of *all* the human resource managers in the greater Miami area. In short, it's a coup, and when I walked into that office I was bound and determined to come out of it a winner.

In addition to my game face and my most winsome smile, I've got on my best old suit—vintage chic, I like to call it—a new tie, and a pair of nice but equally worn leather shoes I've repaired with super glue and duct tape.

But more significant than any of that was the trick I had up my sleeve.

Human resource managers are notoriously overworked and underpaid and this manager, in particular, seemed more burned out than most.

No worries, I assured myself. I was confident I could charm her.

She was plump, in her late thirties, no wedding band. She'd pushed her hair away from her round face with a wide headband and the eyes behind her especially thick glasses were bored and disinterested, the hallmark of the post-lunch carb-induced stupor. A quick look at her desk revealed a couple of personal photos—a pair of children, the other a dog—and a tidy, organized person who liked cocker spaniels and jelly beans.

It was a start.

"Good afternoon, Patricia. Thanks so much for seeing me today."

"You're welcome," she sighed without looking at me, her attention aimed at her desktop as she nudged it out of sleep mode.

"Aw," I said, glancing at one of the pictures, determined to engage her. "You have adorable kids. How old are they?" People, in my experience, loved to talk about their children.

"Five and nine. But they're not mine, they're my sister's." Her face crumpled. "I can't h-have ch-children," she added brokenly. "Bad uterus. My husband couldn't handle it. He left me three weeks ago."

I blinked, stunned. This was entirely too much personal information and, admittedly, my brain is ill-equipped to handle these sorts of emotional issues. It sorts information into three categories—"interesting," "useful" and my personal favorite ,"problem to be solved."

There's no silo for sad—I don't know what to do with it.

"I, uh…"

"I'm sorry," she interrupted, taking a fortifying breath. "That was unprofessional." She massaged the bridge of her nose. "Remind me again why you're here."

Fabulous. I've already fumbled with the kid question and she doesn't even know what our appointment is about. I could see this meeting circling the drain with much more rapidity than I was prepared for. If Mike didn't radio in the next two minutes it would be too late.

"I'm Francisco Guerra with Bombino Brothers Entertainment Troupe. We offer a full-service—"

"Ah, right," she said. "I remember now." Unhappily, by the look on her face. "Listen, Mr. Guerra, we've got a good relationship with Sam's Friends and Festivities and I don't think—"

Thankfully, my radio went off before she could finish giving me the kiss of death speech.

"Fran to Mike?"

"Excuse me," I said, inspecting the display. "I've been waiting for this call. Mike," I said, relieved for more than one reason. "Please tell me the elephants have arrived."

Patricia's dim eyes flared with the first bit of interest.

"Yes, they're here," Mike confirmed, the hint of laughter in his voice only discernible to me.

I breathed an affected enormous sigh of relief, purely for Patricia's benefit. "Fantastic," I said. "What about the midget?"

Silence yawned for an uncomfortable beat—probably because Mike was staring goggled-eyed at the radio, I imagined—then "Yes, there are two of them actually. Twins. Pork and Bean. And they brought their trained goats and the blind albino python."

It was all I could do to keep a straight face. Mike had gone off script, but I couldn't fault his improv skills. You see, we uh, didn't exactly have access to elephants or twin midgets with trained goats and a blind albino python. We were a small operation that needed more business in order to grow…but to get that business we needed to *look* like we were a big operation.

Despite one more misstep when I asked about her dog—"I had to put him down last week," she'd said, in tears once again. "I held his paw and sang the "Circle of Life"—I ultimately walked out of her office with her company's business and, just as I'd known, that connection led to dozens of others which made Bombino Brothers a force to be reckoned with. I sold the business a few years later for a tidy profit.

The lesson here? Be strategic, and don't be afraid to go big or go home.

While most businessmen will tell you that the shotgun approach is best, I've always found a rifle shot to be more effective. I used *one* big company to garner the business of *lots* of others. It was a targeted, effective approach.

When looking for markets to sell your product, go to the biggest source first, then work your way down. For instance, when I patented the snow machine I knew that the film and entertainment business would hold the largest pool of potential clients, so I started there first. From there I contacted any venue with entertainment—theatres, night clubs, ice skating rinks, malls.

I'll never forget when we were pitching to Cirque du Soleil in Montreal, home of their Canadian headquarters. We'd set up outside and, as it happened, it was snowing. When we brought our machine into the building and demonstrated *our* snow, management was blown away. They hadn't been able to tell a difference between our snow and the original, and Canadians are pretty well-versed when it comes to frozen precipitation, let me tell you.

Another way to concentrate your resources is to attend trade shows. Practically every global business has its own association and holds yearly trade shows where like-minded vendors come in, set up and demonstrate their products to representatives and buyers who have the power to bring your product into their arsenal of inventory.

Instead of traveling all over the country hosting your presentation over and over again, do it as many times as necessary while potential clients come to *you*. Save time *and* money. This is a streamlined, cost-effective approach with maximum visibility for a relatively low cost. It's a limited investment with the potential for a great return.

In other words, *strategic*.

Additionally, considering writing articles for publications which cater to your desired clientele, then place small ads in those same publications—a targeted approach. Don't waste your time or money putting ads for your new tractor supply gadget in fashion magazines. Consider the Farmer's Almanac instead. Makes better sense, right?

Trust me, this isn't complicated. It's *smart*. It's utilizing time and money to your best advantage, one that will hopefully pay off in licensing and sales dollars. That's the goal, remember?

And listen, I know that I've said this before, but it bears repeating—these people *want* to meet you.

They're all looking for new and innovative ways to improve their own customer experience. They all want to be trendsetters, ahead of the curve—not behind it—and if you've got a product that can do that, then ninety percent of your work is done.

It's just a matter of getting the *right* product in front of the *right* people.

Did everyone I presented the snow machine to want it? No, obviously not. While admittedly most of them were impressed—it's an excellent invention, after all—and could see the value and viability of it, not everyone was interested in implementing the machine as part of their entertainment experience. And, of course, those people were stupid.

Ha! Just kidding.

The point? Don't be discouraged, kid. Not everyone is going to want what you have, but that doesn't mean that it isn't marketable—it only means you've got to try harder to find the *right* market. And, ultimately, you will.

Concentrate your resources, make the most of your time, money and energy. This is a marathon, not the fifty yard dash.

Be *smart*.

Be *strategic*.

And don't be afraid to beat your chest and roar when necessary. Sometimes you've got to pull an elephant from your sleeve and a midget out of your hat to get to where you want to go. The road to the top is often bumpy and filled with pot holes, but I can promise you this—it's never boring and it's *never* a disappointment.

Buckle up, kid, and enjoy the ride.

STEP SIX: BE PERSISTENT—NARROW
THE GAP

"Flaming enthusiasm, backed up by horse sense and persistence, is the quality that most frequently makes for success." —Dale Carnegie

You know that one person who hounds the hell out of you about going to the gym, or volunteering at the church bazaar or just basically tries to either get you to do something you don't want to do, or sell you something you don't want to buy? Know how you cringe when your see their number pop up on your Caller ID? How the sound of their voice is reminiscent of fingernails down a chalk board or unexpected feedback from a microphone?

Yeah. We've all got one, don't we? *Don't* be that guy.

There's a difference between being unapologetically persistent and tactlessly annoying. I find that this most often happens when the person I'm dealing with has developed end-goal tunnel vision. Targeted determination is a wonderful thing and I firmly believe that every good businessman should have it, but that doesn't mean that practical communication skills aren't still in effect.

It's good to believe in yourself, to believe in your product, to be totally all in and sold out to the future success you envision, but part of that future has to include common courtesy—which, sadly, isn't quite so common anymore—and the ability to work well with others. In a world where stress levels are at an all-time high and everyone is looking for ways to weed unnecessary tension from their lives, the last thing you want to be is an unwelcome dandelion cluttering up someone's designer sod.

Be assessable. Be easy-going. Let your product do the talking.

Remember, all new business is based on *new* ideas.

These executives aren't vaudeville villains sitting behind their desks tweaking their evil mustaches. They're dedicated professionals who are looking for ways to increase their bottom line. The idea that they're hidden away in ivory towers or behind locked doors with limited access is simply a myth and, while it's certainly okay to utilize social media and various professional web sites like LinkedIn to make the connections you need to make, sometimes the good old-fashioned approach works best.

Just pick up the phone and call.

Emails are too easily deleted or ignored—I've got staff who sorts through mine. Just *call.* If you're not comfortable doing that, then that's all the more reason you should. Good phone skills are a *must.* As a matter of fact, that's how I got the snow machine into the theme parks. I simply picked up the phone, politely asked the receptionist the name of the special effects director and you know what?

She gave it to me. Simple as that.

Armed with his name, I disconnected and called back, then asked for him. Wonder of wonders he was at his desk. Can you believe it?

"Hi, Mr. Kelly, my name is Francisco Guerra. I've developed a new special effects product I'd like to show you. Would you have time for a demonstration? I'd love to bring it by." I gave him a brief description of my snow machine.

"Sounds promising," he told me. "I'd love to see it."

Two days later I took my snow machine on site, met with Mr. Kelly and proceeded to show him what it could do. No fancy power point slides, no board room meeting—just me and my product. Simple, streamlined and efficient. Guess what? Turns out the park was in need of a snow machine that would produce evaporative snow that wouldn't leave a slick residue or surface, and two months later was installing $150,000 worth of equipment in one of the most beloved theme parks in the world. That single phone call netted me an instant significant return, opened the door into the theme park market and resulted in a twenty-plus year relationship with those companies.

Initiative and a good product—you simply can't beat that combination.

Does that mean that you're not going to hit the occasional road block? No, of course not. But when that happens, just get creative. I can't tell you how many times I've used the "I'm-writing-an-article" ruse to my advantage.

I'm-writing-an-article ruse? But, Fran, isn't that dishonest? *Well...* Okay, yeah, maybe, in the strictest sense of the word, but I prefer to think of it as "resourceful communication."

Dale Carnegie says "Talk to someone about themselves and they'll listen for hours." And you know what?

He's right.

People *love* to talk about themselves. You call up the head of a research and development department at a company—let's call him Dwight—and ask him why he chose a specific product, I can promise he's going to tell you. In detail and with enthusiasm. Ahhhh. Did you feel that breeze? That's the window of opportunity opening up. Crawl on through it and plant your feet firmly on the ledge.

"You know, as it happens, Dwight, I'm an inventor as well and I've got something I think you'll be interested in…"

I've got a buddy who owns a web design business who actually used this technique to grow his business. He and his partner were spending so much time slinging code they didn't have time to dedicate to sales. They were maintaining the business, but not growing it and, despite multiple marketing attempts, couldn't seem to reach that next level.

"Fran, I don't know what else to do," Al confided. "My well of good ideas seems to have gone dry."

I recommended the I'm-writing-an-article approach. "Target web sites that are in desperate need of an overhaul," I said.

Albert was uncomfortably quiet for a moment. "Let me get this straight. You want me to call up these companies, tell them that I'm writing an article and would like to ask their permission to use their web site as an example—"

"Of what not to do," I interjected. "Tell them how terrible their web site is, how it's the best example of what *not* to do, ever."

Another lengthy silence. "Um, right."

"Trust me."

His hesitation screamed across the line. "I don't know, Fran. I—"

"*Trust me.* They're going to ask you what's wrong with their web site and then you'll be able to offer a solution to their problem. Nobody wants to be used as a poor example for anything."

A week later I get a call from Al. "You were right."

Ah. Be still my heart. My three most favorite words.

"Business is booming," he went on. "I've hired a sales rep who does nothing but cold call poorly designed sites. You know, Fran, I've got to admit I had my doubts, but… Wow. It's fantastic. I can't thank you enough."

Of course, I was right. I usually am, after all. "A fifth of Gentleman Jack will do."

Is the above-referenced approach always the best? Obviously not, but if you've exhausted all other potential avenues, then certainly give it a shot. Nothing ventured, nothing gained and the risk is definitely worth the reward.

The most important thing to always keep in mind is to never give up, because you never know what's going to work, when that phone call is going to get answered, that email returned, when a cold contact will suddenly burn hot.

Years ago I was visiting a coastal city in California and had gone for a walk when I came upon a statue of a man feeding seagulls. I'd heard the story about the statue and the man depicted in it before--I'm sure lots of people have--but as luck would have it, further down the beach I actually happened upon him. Amazing, right?

"That's you, isn't it?" I said, gesturing back toward the statue.

The old man looked up at me and smiled, his weathered face a testament to many years and a life well-lived. He nodded. "It is," he said, tossing another handful of fish out of his bucket. The birds swooped in and out, plucking the food as much from the air as the ground.

"Wow," I said, for lack of anything better. "You must feed the seagulls quite often."

"Every day for the past forty-eight years," he told me.

Shock detonated through me and I felt my eyebrows climb toward my hairline. *Every day? For the past forty-eight years?* "Really?"

He nodded again, chuckled low at my expression. "Really."

Admittedly, that was impressive. I couldn't commit to a workout schedule for more than a month and this guy has been feeding seagulls every day for nearly *fifty* years? Wow. Just wow. Talk about dedication. I wanted to hear the story first-hand, so I waited, hoping my patience would be rewarded.

It was.

"Yeah, well, a single seagull saved my life and the life of the men under my command a half century ago, so it's my way of saying thanks, I guess."

"You're a vet?"

"World War II. Navy. We took a hit, had to abandon ship and managed to climb into a sad little life boat with too little room and no food or water. Floated out there for days beneath the blistering sun. You want to know the measure of a man, son?" he said, shooting me a look. "Face death with him and you'll find out pretty damned quick. I'll tell you, we were nearing the end, had just about had all we could stand. We were dehydrated, starving. Slowly, painfully dying and were all contemplating suicide, myself included," he added, shooting me a look. "Miles and miles of ocean, not a single bit of land in sight, not a single boat, plane...nothing. I kept telling them that I was certain that they were looking for us, that they'd find us, but the truth was I'd just about decided that the military had concluded that we'd all gone down with the ship, and that there wasn't a rescue party combing that bit of ocean at all."

I shook my head. I couldn't even begin to imagine that kind of danger, much less predict how I'd behave should I ever find myself in the same situation.

"So there we were," he went on. "Trying to decide how we were going to do it—how we were going to end our own lives—when out of nowhere—*literally nowhere*—a single seagull suddenly lit on the side of the boat. They're never alone, seagulls," he added. "Think about that. They always travel in, at the very least, pairs. And yet here was one, miles and miles from land, in a place it shouldn't be. We all froze, didn't so much as breathe. And then I grabbed it." He calmly tossed out more fish. "We shared that raw bird and it was just enough to restore our spirits and our failing bodies and two days later we were rescued."

More in awe than I could have ever imagined, I passed a hand over my face and glanced at him. "That's... Wow, that's incredible."

He just smiled, lifted a shoulder. "That's hope for you," he said. "I've been to that awful place where it vanishes like a spent match in the darkness, and I feed these birds every day as a reminder that I don't ever want to go back."

It's been fifteen or more years since I had that conversation with that old man and yet every second of it is embedded in my memory. I've met lots of people from all different walks of life since meeting him, and I can tell you that there hasn't been a message that's been any more significant or profound.

Never give up, fan that flame of hope as though your life depends on it—even if it doesn't because you never know when it *might*—and be thankful for every good turn that comes your way, because you never know what could be just around the corner.

Be patiently persistent and I'll promise you this, kid—your seagull moments will come, too. You can bet on it.

STEP SEVEN: LICENSING—THE ULTIMATE MONEY-MAKER

"Half of Google's revenue comes from text-based ads that are placed near search results and are related to the topic of the search. Another half of its revenues come from licensing its search technology to companies like Yahoo."—Eric Schmidt

Next to actually creating my inventions and seeing the patents, this is probably the part of the process that I get the most excited about. Do you know why? Because if we were watching *Jerry McGuire*, this would be Cuba Gooding, Jr.'s infamous "Show Me the Money" scene.

This is where the rubber meets the road, kid. This is where every bit of your ingenuity and entrepreneurial skills actually *pays* off. It's that special moment when the inventor's creation is introduced into the commercial market, where creativity meets commerce, where those things ultimately culminate in lots of dollar bills in your bank account.

This is also one of those things that, on the surface, appears very complicated—and certainly there are aspects of it that can be to the uneducated—but ultimately…it's not.

The truth is we all license *every* day.

Every time you check the "I agree" box on a "terms of

service" agreement for software, you're licensing.

When you download music, you're licensing.

When you rent or lease something, you're licensing. In exchange for payment, you're agreeing to rent or use something that someone else owns.

In its basest, truest form *that's* licensing.

The only thing that changes is the variables. For example, the length of the agreement, who's responsible for what, how payment will be made, what happens if the agreement is broken, etc... Those sorts of things.

In a nutshell, licensing simply gives someone the right to make, distribute and sell an invention. Provided you've followed the steps to this point, this is where you are in the process and as such, here are a few things you need to know.

Number one—a large advance isn't always in your best interest. Yes, yes, I know that this seems to fly in the face of convention, but hear me out. Depending on your invention and how much it's going to cost to produce, in many cases, a large advance against royalties leaves the licensor too little money in reserve for research and development.

Guess what, chief? That's not good for you.

The whole purpose of your invention is to get it to market—to sell it. If there's not enough money left in the budget to actually put your product on the shelves, then that defeats the point, right? You might have banked a large advance, but how much did you lose in sales revenue?

Remember I said I netted a fifty-thousand dollar advance for my first snow machine? I did, that's true. But what's also true is that the next year the company I'd licensed my technology to filed for bankruptcy. I didn't have to return the advance—it was nonrefundable—but the second year I didn't receive that advance and I ultimately had to look for another licensor for my product.

Lesson learned. Another example of my hindsight being your twenty-twenty.

Number two—make sure that your product doesn't get "shelved," meaning that you're invention has simply been purchased by the licensor with the intent to keep it from going to market as competition for other products. You want retail sales, not just money. Longevity, remember? You're building a brand here—You, Inc—and every invention that you add to your inventory is an asset.

Number three—always let the licensor initiate the offer. *Always*. As a general rule, when it comes to inventions, industry standard royalty rates against *wholesale*—not retail— are anywhere from three to five percent.

That's it.

Believe it or not, there are people who are convinced that they should get anywhere from twenty to thirty percent and, in my twenty plus year career in this business, I have *never* seen that happen. Not even once. I'm not saying it *can't* happen because as sure as I do, I'll get a phone call or an email from someone who did manage to get that sort of percentage.

"You were wrong, Fran—my least favorite words in the English language. Thankfully I don't hear them very often— my good friend so-and-so got a forty percent royalty rate *and* a dozen Crusty Crème donuts for life!" Fantastic for her. I hope she got a lifetime gym membership as well. Again, not saying it can't happen. I'm just saying that I think I've got a better chance of spotting Big Foot in my back yard.

But here's the thing about waiting for an offer. Occasionally you'll come across a company who will offer eight or nine percent, and that's certainly a better rate of return. Should they happen to come in below industry standard, then cite the standard and negotiate for better terms.

Number four—never give anyone exclusivity unless it's at a premium. Every once in a while I'll give a company a head start—a six to twelve month lead—but ultimately, my goal is to sell as many items as I can, and limiting my distributors isn't in my best interests or better for my bottom line. If possible, avoid subject of exclusivity altogether. It's better if the subject doesn't come up.

Number five—attorneys aren't always the best source for negotiating licensing agreements. Lawyers are in the business of arguing, not deal making. Better to use an experienced licensing agent—like myself, hint, hint, nudge, nudge—or someone of equal caliber.

Ultimately, though, this is something that you need to learn how to do for yourself.

Why? Because who better to protect your interests than yourself? It's another arrow of skill to add to your quiver, another ace—or elephant, as the case may be—up your sleeve. Better still, it's a necessary skill for the *inventor*preneur.

Ultimately, every serious inventor needs to know how to negotiate a good license agreement. It's as simple as that.

Here's the deal. To some degree, I think we all have some fear and trepidation when it comes to the unknown, and that is certainly the case when embarking on this particular career path. But if you've made it this far—if you're smart enough to either improve an existing product or create something completely new—then you are definitely smart enough to learn how to do this.

I've said it before and I'll say it again—it's not that hard. It's really not.

Are you going to make mistakes? Yes, definitely. Lord knows I did. But you *will* recover, and the next time you'll take that experience with you and you'll get a little bit better. And a little bit better, and a little bit better.

In all probability, you'll make a *different* mistake each time, but that's okay, kid, so long as you learn from them.

STEP EIGHT: CLOSE THE DEAL—WRAPPING IT UP

"Success is a science; if you have the conditions you get the results."—Oscar Wilde

So you've found your passion, you've identified the market, you've secured your intellectual property, you've prepared your presentation, you've strategically and persistently isolated potential interested parties, you're in the process of negotiating the license agreement and you're ready to close the deal.

After months—possibly *years*—of hard work, you've successfully found an interested party to help move your invention to market.

Up until this point things have been in high gear—boom, done, boom, done, boom, done. You've been hustling, ticking boxes, not just making sure that all of your ducks are in a row, but that they're color coordinated and arranged by size and shape, so it's going to feel really strange now when everything slows to a crawl.

This part, strangely, is very anticlimactic.

Don't panic. This is normal. The other side has retreated to its corner to consider the upfront royalties—the guaranteed minimum—and the cost to bring your product to market. Reasonable, right? After all, they're in this to make money as well. They're not doing it out of the goodness of their heart. This is business, not charity, but because it's business you need to get them to push on, to actually *close* the deal. The sooner the agreement is signed, the sooner both parties can start making money.

A word of caution. Most retailers are hesitant to deal with a one-product company. Say your admittedly brilliant invention doesn't find traction in the market and the retailer has to initiate a mark down to move the inventory. If you don't have another item in the pipeline, then where is that mark-down cost going to get made up? How is the retailer supposed to recoup his money?

He can't.

If you're a one-off inventor—if you've simply, by necessity, invented a new product to aid another or have found a way to improve an existing process—then consulting someone like me, who has an established a track record and is a retailer as well, is probably your best bet. It's also why you're reading this book.

Because I'm a retailer as well, I'll often scroll through patents to look for new technology, but I actually think that I'm the exception to the rule. (I generally am, just ask me.) For the most part, just because you've filed a patent doesn't mean people are going to start beating down your door. You've got to go out and find those doors and if you can't find one, then build one.

Opportunity and initiative—you're not going to find better partners.

Additionally, if you've created a new invention or process and you're presenting it as an "outsider"—someone not in house or affiliated with that particular company—then you can typically expect some push back. People can often get very territorial, especially when it's possibly something that should have been developed in house. No one wants to be shown up, as it were.

Consider this. After Christopher Columbus returned from the Americas to Spain, he was meeting with Queen Isabella and members of her parliament, petitioning to mount another expedition. Many of the members of parliament were skeptical, but there was one, in particular, who was very antagonistic.

"You ran into a large area of land," he scoffed. "How hard can it be?"

Don't you know old Chris wanted to knock the smirk off that guy's face? Can you imagine having that sort of accomplishment reduced to something so trivial and insignificant by someone who'd, in all probability, never set foot on a *real* ship, much less aimed it into uncharted waters?

Think about that for a moment and imagine the bravery, the determination, the sheer unadulterated *nerve* it took those early explorers to climb into those boats and set off. Astounding, isn't it? Particularly when you consider how dependent we've become as a society on the GPS programs loaded onto our smart phones.

But that's the thing, right? Lots of things can *appear* easy after someone else has done them.

No doubt Columbus was irritated, but rather than allow the exchange to devolve into an argument, he looked at the man, pointed to a platter of hard boiled eggs on the buffet table behind him and politely asked him to hand him a couple.

Bewildered, the man agreed.

Columbus held up an egg for all to see. "I can make this egg stand on its end. Can you?"

The man's eyes widened in disbelief, then he smiled, convinced that if Columbus could do it, then he could, too. "Certainly," he told him. He accepted the challenge, walked over to the table and tried several times to get the egg to stand on end, first one, then the other. When the egg had rolled over for the fifth time, the man threw up his hands in frustration and said, "No, it's not possible!"

While the rest of the room watched in rapt attention,

Columbus merely arched a brow, strolled over to the table, put his egg down, then pushed it until the bottom flattened, allowing the egg to stand on its end, as promised.

"No!" the man exploded. "You've cheated! It was a trick!"

"It was not a trick," Columbus told him. "But now that I've shown you how to do it, it's easy, isn't it?"

Needless to say, Columbus was granted funding for another expedition.

More recently I had another friend who found himself in a similar situation and who actually cited the Columbus story to illustrate his point. Imagine this. It's the early nineties and cell phone technology is really taking off. Interestingly enough, this new technology was impacting the prison systems in a negative way more than any other.

Prison, Fran? Really?

Yes, *really*. Think about it. The bulk of prison revenue comes from the pay phones installed to facilitate communication between inmates and the outside world. But in addition to the cell phones being illegally introduced into the prisons, the actual telephones were causing problems as well because inmates were using the handset to assault other prisoners—bashing them over the head, choking them with the cord, etc…

At the time, my friend was called in to come up with a solution for the prison systems. Remember, they're bleeding money, swiftly moving into the red. Everyone is all up in arms, the melodrama is in high gear and everyone is on edge.

"Can you offer a solution?" they asked my friend, Dario.

Dario was quiet for a moment, then smiled. "Yes, I can," he told them. "I'll be back tomorrow with a prototype."

The next morning the group reassembled and, if possible, the tension was higher, tempers were even worse. Dario strolled in, pulled a telephone handset with a *drastically* shorter cord from a bag and laid it on the table.

"Really?" one of the men scoffed. "*That's* your solution? *That's* your answer to our problem? *Jesus.*" He rolled his eyes, muttered a curse under his breath.

"It is," Dario told him. "Sometimes the solution to the most difficult problem is the simplest one." Inmates wouldn't be able to use the phone or the cord as a weapon if it wasn't long enough to actually *make* it one.

It was a *brilliantly simple* solution and no one in the room with the exception of Dario had thought of it.

You, too, can occasionally expect some push back. It's human nature and there's always going to be someone who is skeptical of your invention. If this happens, it's been my experience that addressing the elephant in the room is the best approach. Call them out, tell them to put any animosity aside and to look for common ground, or you'll go over their head. Because you know who doesn't care where a good idea comes from, so long as it's better for the company?

The CEO.

To that end, historically, I've found that dealing with a single decision maker is much better than working with a committee—you often run into the too many chiefs and not enough Indians syndrome—and it's just a simpler, more efficient process. Rather than waiting on a vote or a consensus, you're waiting on a single answer and it's the one that counts.

Ultimately, though, nothing is going to sell your product more than the product itself. In 2008 I co-invented floating clouds which could be shaped into logos—*Flogos*, we named them. Clever, yes? These clouds can travel anywhere from two-thousand to thirty-thousand feet in the air, they're totally biodegradable and completely green.

In short, they're *amazing*. Just ask me and I tell you so.

When we first successfully developed the technology, rather than shop it around the usual channels, I opted to let the media do the work for me. I simply put together a press release and sent it to the Associated Press. "Small Alabama firm makes floating clouds into the shapes of logos." I included the bit about them being biodegradable and green and within a week and a half, more than a million articles had been written about our product.

As such I negotiated a licensing agreement for *Flogos* with twenty-three different countries and propelled our little Alabama business into the global market. From there, my distributors did the rest. Featured at amusement parks, sporting events, corporate events and even movie premieres, our *Flogos* have seen world-wide success.

That's how you close a deal, kid, and it's an *exhilarating* ride.

STEP NINE: PROTECTING YOUR INTERESTS—YOU'RE JUST GETTING STARTED

"Your reputation is worth more than your paycheck and your integrity is worth more than your career."—Ryan Freitas

This step is more common sense than anything else, but it bears covering because it's *so* important.

I'm sure that you've heard the old adage that you only get one chance to make a first impression. I know that it sounds trite, but did you know that research shows that first impressions are generally made in the first tenth of a second? *The first tenth of a second.*

Think about that. The next time you're introduced to someone, think about how quickly you decided whether or not you liked them, whether you thought they were trustworthy, attractive, honest, interesting. The first impression is also the longest-lasting and the memory of that meeting is one that's difficult to overcome should you make a bad impression.

To give you an idea of what I mean and how important these things are, I'm going to tell you a story. In my very early 20's, I was a struggling magician. I was working my butt off, but couldn't seem to get any real traction. Frankie was a baby, I had responsibilities and the general attitude from my family was that I was wasting my time doing the magician bit, that I should man-up, get a "real" job.

But I loved what I was doing and I knew that there was a future in it—I *knew* it—and I knew that if I could just catch one big break that I'd be on my way. Luckily, I had a friend who believed in me, too, and he'd heard about an interview for an ad campaign for the Nabisco company.

The audition was taking place in New York and he'd secured an appointment for me.

Against advice from almost everyone I knew, I took the last bit of money I had and bought a two-hundred dollar plane ticket to the Big Apple. The morning my flight was supposed to leave my car wouldn't start and a neighbor had to drive me to the airport. I've got forty bucks in my pocket—just enough for cabs back and forth into Midtown and my lunch—my bag of tricks, and butterflies the size of mutant hummingbirds in my belly. Ask anyone who knows me and they'll tell you that confidence is something I've never been terribly short on. (Not always true, but I can fake it with the best of them.)

That morning I was shaking in my shoes. I was utterly terrified. Every negative thing I'd heard about why this was a waste of time and a bad idea, every bit of "practical" advice was ringing in my ears.

I made it into the city, made my way over to the office building where the interviews were being conducted just to familiarize myself and to let the receptionist know that I'd arrived. One look into that room and my already shaky bravado took another lethal hit.

Everyone who was anyone in my field was there. All the big guys, the ones who'd been at this much longer than I had been, who were making considerably more money than I was. And to make matters even worse, my *arch* enemy—yes, I'm using comic book language—was there, too.

He smirked.

I fled.

I decided to take the time to once again go through my act, make sure that everything was as it should be and grab some lunch. I went to Burger King, because it was close and it was cheap, and the cab had cost more than I'd expected. Once I'd finished up and it was time to make my way back for my interview, I'd walked outside and was waiting for the light to change when it happened.

The instant the pedestrian walk sign illuminated, people bolted from the safety of the sidewalk like horses from behind the gate and, across the street, I watched in dismay as an older gentleman was knocked down, landing hard in the icy sludge the city streets were notorious for during that time of year. His briefcase went in one direction, he went in the other, and—this is the part that gets me every time—not a *single* person stopped to help him. They dodged him, stepped over him, damn near *tripped* over him, but no one—*no one*— offered a helping hand.

I did, of course, because that's just me.

In the first place, it's common courtesy. In the second, my father had been the custodian of a retirement village since moving to the States and, as such, I had a deeper respect and appreciation for senior citizens. Amazing what you can learn from people who actually have life experience, but that's another story.

Back to this one.

So I finally get to him, I reach down and help him up, then quickly snag his soaked brief case and hand it over.

He thanked me, rather gruffly—embarrassed, I imagined--and then took off.

When I looked down, I was a mess. A *mess*. My white shirt was stained with dirty water, my pants were wet from the knees down, my tie was soaked.

And my interview was in fifteen minutes.

Desperate to try to salvage the appointment, I hurried back across the street to Burger King, had rinsed my shirt out and was drying it beneath the hand dryer when the manager came in and threw me out. He assumed I was a vagrant. I was carrying a bag and doing my laundry in his bathroom, so it was a fair assumption.

By the time I got back to the office building the lobby was deserted, I was ten minutes late, and the receptionist looked at me like I'd rolled in something she would unhappily scrape off the bottom of her shoe.

Yes, things were going splendidly.

With a skeptical once over, she stood and showed me into the adjoining room. It was huge, lots of rich carpet, dark wood and an enviable view of Central Park framed in the window, just like some of the shows I'd seen on TV. From my vantage point, I could see the back of a leather chair, the barest top of a gray head, and a pair of expensive shoes propped up on the credenza behind the desk. My interviewer was on the phone and, as the receptionist showed me my chair, she actually *shushed* me, like I was school boy who'd been called on the carpet for being disruptive.

My cheeks burned.

A couple of minutes ticked by and he remained on the phone, then another and another, and in that time every doubt I'd heard from someone else or allowed into my own head crept in.

This was a waste of time. What was I doing here? I can't believe I spent that money on a plane ticket. What the hell had I been thinking...

I started playing the countdown game in my head. Backward from ten to one and when I reached one, if he wasn't off the phone I was leaving. I was going to go back to Florida with my tail between my legs and get a job in IT somewhere. I'd always been good with computers. I played the game twice and was on the third round when I'd finally committed to leaving.

Six...

This was ignorant.

Five...

If I left now I would have time to check out the Statue of Liberty before going to the airport.

Four…

Looking at it was free. I didn't have to take the tour.

Three…

I should have listened to my father.

Two…

Okay, that's it. I'm out of here.

I just put my hands on either side of the arms of the chair to brace myself to get up when suddenly the feet dropped off the credenza, the phone landed in the cradle and the chair spun around.

It was the old man I'd stop to help up off the street.

I couldn't have been any more shocked if my hair had suddenly burst into flames.

To this day I don't know if I was the best qualified person for the job or if, after his mishap, he'd canceled all the other appointments and I merely got an audience by chance, but I landed that coveted position.

Two-hundred-and-fifty-thousand dollars a year.

"Ultimately, this job is all about character," he told me. "And I know you've got it."

First impressions, kid. Make them count.

Don't pull a bait and switch—always deliver what you promise—and be accessible when it comes to helping the company manufacture your product. I can't tell you how many times I've actually helped place inventors on company payrolls as independent consultants, making on average one-hundred-and-twenty-five thousand dollars a year. As I've mentioned before, the inventor inevitably becomes the master and his expertise is invaluable.

You will ultimately form a connection with that company, in all probability, become friends with its owner. You're building lasting relationships, trust, and accountability. Peter Rocheleau, the current President of Global Home Products, was actually with Bradford Novelty, the first company who ever distributed my snow machine. When the business closed a year later, Peter came on board with me and we've been working together now for nearly twenty years. Many, many millions under the bridge.

That's what you want—partnerships, a professional network of people you can count on—and the way to build that is by doing what you say, delivering what you promise, being accessible and willing to help, and offering top-notch customer service.

Easy concepts, not always an easy follow-through, but always, *always* worth it, kid. Make the effort. Trust me on this.

STEP TEN: WHEN ALL ELSE FAILS—THE DIY APPROACH

"The value of an idea lies in the using of it."—*Thomas Edison*

Every once in a while an inventor will create something that is utterly phenomenal, has tremendous value, but despite his or her best efforts, can't successfully get it to market. In those cases, it becomes necessary for the inventor to become the manufacturer *and* the distributer. This is where those *inventor*preneur skills are really going to come into play. This is where you become a bonafide contender, a force to be reckoned with, the gunslinger with the biggest pistol. Well, maybe not a *real* gunslinger, Little Joe, but you get the idea.

This scenario actually happened to me once with my date rape drug detector. You might remember back in early 2002 that date rape drugs were rampant in nightclubs, resulting in a near-epidemic of women being sexually victimized. I actually knew a woman that this happened to and it inspired me to come up with a solution, a way for women to protect themselves.

What came about was a coaster with two color chromatic indicators which would signify the presence of drugs, if found. Simply place a drop in the designated area and if any drugs were detected, the spot would turn blue much in the same way as pregnancy tests. It took seconds.

Convinced that I had a needed preventive product that

could literally save lives, I hired a licensing agent and put him to work. Two months later?

Nothing. Nada. Zilch. He couldn't get anywhere.

At this point, I decided to manufacture and distribute the invention myself—it literally cost pennies to make, so not only was it a really excellent product, I thought it was an inexpensive way for night club owners to protect their clientele. (Night club owners thought it was socially unacceptable to insult the men who were buying the drinks for the women by implying that they were potential rapist, so ultimately they didn't agree, but I digress...)

Ultimately I manufactured the coasters myself and stocked them into all the major drugstores—Walgreens, CVS, Rite Aid, etc...and then I put out another press release.

Unsurprisingly, the news garnered national attention.

The *Miami Herald* picked it up first and it resulted in one-hundred thousand stories. That's when the manufacturers started calling me, particularly those in the wine and spirits industries. One company was especially keen, offered me two-million dollars. We shook hands and popped the champagne.

Two days later I got a call from them and they backed out. Their attorneys didn't think it was a good idea to get involved in the problem with date rape.

No worries, I thought. Another company quickly stepped up with an even better offer. Shook hands and popped the champagne again and guess what? Two days later another set of attorneys mounted the same argument. The deal fell through. Can you believe it?

Because I was determined to see this succeed, we came up with the ingenious idea to sell advertising on the coasters into the local bars and nightclubs and the product took off. We produced millions of them, basically eradicated the date rape drug craze, worked with local law enforcement there in Miami. The product was featured on Oprah Winfrey, Larry King, *Time Magazine*, *Newsweek*.

Arguably one of the most successful inventions I've ever had and I couldn't get anyone—*anyone*—to touch it. I kept the company for ten years, then sold it for an excellent profit.

The lesson, kid? Just because you can't get someone to move your product doesn't mean that it's bad. Sometimes you've just got to don every hat—inventor, manufacturer, distributer—and do it yourself.

While I will say that, ideally, strictly working on the licensing side is a lot less involved and certainly nets more cash, occasionally there will be inventions that come up that not only allow you to entertain or help people, but genuinely impact a particular problem. Those are the ones worth fighting for because those are the ones that will ultimately result in your legacy.

Each and everyone one of my inventions, from my snow machine, to my other special effects designs, to my *Flogos*, to my date rape drug detector… They're all a piece of my legacy, but the ones that really stick with you are the ones that you believed in and fought for, when companies that were bigger than you, with more resources at their disposal, *wouldn't*.

That's when you can pat yourself on the back and say, "Wow, you know what? I made a difference. I did something that *really* helped people."

Talk about a trophy moment.

I can only think of one instance when I was prouder and that's when my ultimate legacy, my Frankie, was born. Flesh of my flesh, blood of my blood, my very DNA.

I believe that as citizens of the world we're all called to protect it and make it better for the next generation, but when you look into the face of your child—or any child, really—that conviction takes on a whole new meaning. It lends a sense of purpose, of urgency, of responsibility. It did for me, in any case and, while I am proud of my success, the money and the things I've been able to buy with it, my real sense of self-worth comes from knowing that I'm passing on this knowledge to my son, and to you.

That I'm actually *sharing* a way to build excitement for new ideas, new technology, new innovations—in essence, a blueprint for the inventions of the future, and who knows what kind of a legacy, ultimately, that will create?

The possibilities are mind-bogglingly, excitingly and humbly...endless.

And you know what, kid? So are yours.

Another trophy moment.

Coming in May
SHAKE AND BAKE: Cooking Up A Fortune--
The Francisco Guerra Story

Every once in a while a writer will happen upon a story that grabs them by the throat and won't let go. We live for these stories, these rare instances of creative synergy where the stars align, the muse blesses us and the words pour out so swiftly that the page doesn't so much as capture them as *absorbs* them. It's magical. Validating. Utterly inspired. These stories are almost always our own, incubated in our brains, hatched via our imaginations.

The story that you are about to read isn't one that I pulled from my head and wrote into existence—it's more complicated, more compelling and more inspiring than anything I could make up—and, even though it's not *my* story, it's nonetheless had the same aforementioned effect.

Cuban immigrant, magician to millionaire inventor, Francisco Guerra's story is proof positive that the increasingly elusive and romanticized American Dream is still possible, still attainable to those who don't have Ivy League educations or large trust funds to subsidize their goals. Riddled with lows reminiscent of Greek tragedies, and highs that are nothing short of serendipitous, Francisco's talent for overcoming adversity and his relentless pursuit of success is as heart-warming as it is inspiring, but more than that, it's a well-timed message of hope for the common man...and, as is the case with Francisco, the *not*-so-common man.

Francisco Guerra

**THE FOLLOWING DOCUMENTS ARE
SAMPLES FOR EDUCATIONAL PURPOSES ONLY.
THEY ARE NOT INTENDED AS LEGAL COUNSEL.**

CONFIDENTIAL DISCLOSURE AGREEMENT

Parties: An agreement between ------------------ and ----------
----

Purpose: INCLUDE PROJECT NAME OR TOPIC,
PURPOSE FOR THE DISCUSSIONS AND

The Parties (referred to in this Agreement as "Party" or
"Parties" as appropriate in the context) agree to the
following conditions for the mutual disclosure and
exchange of confidential or proprietary materials and
information, as further defined below, relating to the
Purpose:

1.   "Confidential Information" means all materials
and information provided in a tangible form and marked
as "Confidential" and, if disclosed verbally or in another
non-tangible form, is indicated as Confidential Information
at the time of disclosure and followed, within --------- (
NUMBER) business days after each such disclosure, by
written notice from the disclosing Party identifying the
confidential aspects of the disclosure. TANGIBLE
INFORMATION NEED NOT BE MARKED
CONFIDENTIAL. The Confidential Information may
include, but is not limited to, products, processes,
techniques, know-how, trade secrets, scientific
knowledge, sequences, inventions, data, formulas,

systems, networks, business plans, customer requirements, software, designs, drawings, schematics, sketches, photographs, digital outputs, specifications, documentation, reports, and/or studies, and any copies of the foregoing made by the receiving Party.

2.   In consideration of disclosures under this Agreement, the receiving Party shall neither use Confidential Information disclosed by the other party for any reason other than the Purpose nor provide Confidential Information to any party who is not a signatory to this Agreement without written permission from the disclosing Party. Each Party shall limit disclosure of and access to the other Party's Confidential Information to its employees, including students, research assistants, and postdoctoral fellows for whom such access is necessary for the Purpose, and shall disclose or allow access only to the extent that such individuals have an obligation of confidentiality to the receiving Party. Each Party shall exercise reasonable care to prevent disclosure of Confidential Information to any third party that is not bound by this Agreement.

3. The disclosure period for the exchange of information under this Agreement is for ------ (NUMBER) years after the last date of signature to this Agreement (the ""Disclosure Period"). Upon, or after the expiration of the Disclosure Period, the receiving Party upon request from the disclosing Party shall return any or all Confidential Information to the disclosing Party, except that one copy of Confidential Information may be retained for the sole purpose of determining continuing obligations under this Agreement. Obligations under this Agreement shall terminate five (5) years after the end of

Disclosure Period.

4.   Confidentiality and non-disclosure obligations do not apply to information that:

at the time of the disclosure was generally available to the public or later has becomes generally available to the public through no breach of this Agreement by the receiving Party;

the receiving Party can show by written records was in its possession prior to the time of disclosure and was not acquired, directly or indirectly, from the disclosing Party;

the receiving Party can show by written records was discovered or developed independently, without use or knowledge of the Confidential Information;

the receiving Party can show by written records was obtained from a third party that reasonably believed it was under no obligation of confidentiality or secrecy to the disclosing Party;

is required to be disclosed by law, legal process, government agency, or court order.

5.   Whenever a Party discloses to the other data or technology it knows to be export controlled, it shall separately mark the data or technology "Export Controlled," whether or not the disclosed matter is also marked as "Confidential Information."

6. This Agreement does not create a relationship of agency, partnership, joint venture or license between the Parties. This Agreement does not obligate either Party to purchase anything from or sell anything to the other Party. Nothing in this Agreement shall grant or imply a license or right to use any Confidential Information, or any patents, copyrights, trademarks or trade secrets of the disclosing Party, except to the extent necessary for the Purpose contemplated by this Agreement.

7. Modifications, extensions or amendments to this Agreement shall be effective only if in writing and executed by all Parties to this Agreement. Duly authorized, validly applied electronic signatures are acceptable as original signatures. Any photocopied or electronically produced copy of this fully executed original Agreement shall have the same legal force and effect as a copy of this Agreement that has the original signatures.

8. Disputes arising under this Agreement shall be settled according to appropriate State and/or Federal laws of _____ county in the state of _____ and both parties agree that any and all dispute only be heard in appropriate State and/or Federal Courts of _____ county in the State of _____.

This Agreement shall be executed by all Parties through a duly authorized representative and shall be effective as of the date of last signing.

By: _____

Typed Name:

Date: _____

By: _____

Typed Name:

Title:

Address:

Date: _____

Francisco Guerra

SAMPLE LICENSING AGREEMENT

This agreement is made and entered into between

_____ ,

(hereinafter called **Licensor**) having its principle office/address at

_____

_____,and

_____

_____ (hereinafter called **Licensee**), having its principle office/address at

_____ .

Witnesseth that:

1. Whereas, **Licensor** has the right to grant licenses under the licensed patent rights (as hereinafter defined),and wishes to have the inventions covered by the licensed patent rights in the public interest; and

2. whereas **Licensee** wishes to obtain a license under the licensed patent rights upon the terms & conditions hereinafter set forth:

Now, therefore, in consideration of the premises and the faithful performance of the covenants herein contained it is agreed as follows.

Article I - DEFINITIONS

For the purpose of this agreement, the following definitions shall apply:

1. **Licensed Patent Rights:** Shall mean:

   a. Inventions disclosed in any of Issued Patents and Patent Applications identified herein by, Patent Number and/or Serial Number and country of filing.

   b. Any and all improvements developed by **Licensor,** regardless if the subject of a current patent application, future patent application, or determined to be an improvement, embodiment, or variation in which patent protection is not sought, relating to the **Licensed Patent Rights,** which **Licensor** may now or may hereafter develop, own or control.

   c. Any or all patents, which may issue on patent rights and improvements thereof, developed by **Licensor** and any and all divisions, continuations, continuations-in-part, reissues and extensions of such patents .

2. **Product(s):** Shall mean any materials including, compositions, techniques, devices, methods or inventions relating to or based on the **Licensed Patent Rights**, developed on the date of this agreement or in the future.

3. **Gross Sales:** Shall mean total

_____ (Currency Unit) value(s) of Product(s) FOB manufactured based on the Licensed Patent Rights.

4. **Confidential Proprietary Information:** Shall mean with respect to any Party all scientific, business or financial information relating to such Party, its subsidiaries or affiliates or their respective businesses, except when such information:

    a. Becomes known to the other Party prior to receipt from such first Party;

    b. Becomes publicly known through sources other than such first Party;

    c. Is lawfully received by such other Party from a party other than the first Party; or

    d. Is approved for release by written authorization from such first Party.

5. **Exclusive License:** Shall mean a license, including the right to sublicense, whereby **Licensee**'s rights are sole and entire and operate to exclude all others, including **Licensor** and its affiliates except as otherwise expressly provided herein.

6. **Know-how:** Shall mean any and all technical data, information, materials, trade secrets, technology, formulas, processes, and ideas, including any improvements thereto, in any form in which the foregoing may exist, now owned or co-owned by or exclusively, semi-exclusively or non-exclusively licensed to any party prior to the date of this Agreement or hereafter acquired by any party

during the term of this agreement.

7. **Intellectual Property Rights:** Shall mean any and all inventions, materials, **Know-how**, trade secrets, technology, formulas, processes, ideas or other discoveries conceived or reduced to practices, whether patentable or not.

8. **Royalty (ies):** Shall mean revenues received in the form of cash and/or equity from holdings from **Licensee**s as a result of licensing and using, selling, making, having made, sublicensing or leasing of **Licensed Patent Rights.**

ARTICLE II- GRANT OF EXCLUSIVE /NON-EXCLUSIVE LICENSE

1. **Licensor** hereby grants to **Licensee** the exclusive (worldwide, option to make this non-exclusive) license with the right to sublicense others, to make, have made, use, sell and lease the **Products** described in the **Licensed Patent Rights**.

2. **Licensor** retains the right to continue to use **Licensed Patent Rights** in any way for non-commercial purposes.

ARTICLE III- LICENSE PAYMENTS

1. **Initial payment and royalty rate**. For the licensed herein granted:

    a. **Licensee** agrees to pay an initial (non-refunadble) fee of _____ (   ).

b. **Licensee** shall pay on earned royalty of _____percent (%) of **Licensee**'s **Gross Sales** of **Products** and ------ percent (%) of the sublicensing receipts.

c. **Licensee** shall pay an annual royalty of _____ ( ) for each leased **Product**.

2. **Sublicenses**. The granting and terms of all sublicenses is entirely at **Licensee**'s discretion provided that all sublicenses shall be subjected to the terms and conditions of this agreement.

3. **Minimum royalty: Licensee** will pay **Licensor**, when submitting their royalty report a minimum royalty of _____ (_____) annually.

4. **When a sale is made:** A sale of **Licensed Patent Rights** shall be regarded as being made upon payment for **Products** made using **Licensed Patent Rights**.

5. **Payments:** All sums payable by **Licensee** hereunder shall be paid to **Licensor** in _____ (name of country) and in the currency of the _____ or in U.S. dollars.

6. **Interest:** In the event any royalties are not paid as specified herein, then a compound interest of eighteen percent (18%) shall be due in addition to the royalties accrued for the period of default.

ARTICLE IV - REPORTS, BOOKS AND RECORDS

1. **Reports.** Within thirty (30) days after the end of the

calendar quarter annual period (or as set forth by the parties) during which this agreement shall be executed and delivered within thirty (30) days after the end of each following quarter annual period, **Licensee** shall make a written report to **Licensor** setting forth the **Gross Sales** of **Licensed Patent Rights** sold, leased or used by **Licensee** and total sublicensing receipts during the quarter annual period. If there are no **Gross Sales** or sublicensing receipts, a statement to that effect be made by **Licensee** to **Licensor**. At the time each report is made, **Licensee** shall pay to **Licensor** the royalties or other payments shown by such report to the payable hereunder.

2.   **Books and records. Licensee** shall keep books and records in such   reasonable detail as will permit the reports provided for in Paragraph 1. hereof to be determined. **Licensee** further agrees to permit such books and reports to be inspected and audited by a representative or representatives of **Licensor** to the extent necessary to verify the reports provided for in paragraph 1. hereof; provided, however, that such representative or representatives shall indicate to **Licensor** only whether the reports and royalty paid are correct, if not, the reasons why not.

ARTICLE V - MARKING

Licensee agrees to mark or have marked all **Products** made, used or leased by it or its sublicensees under the **Licensed Patent Rights**, if and to the extent such markings shall be practical, with such patent markings as shall be desirable or required by applicable patent laws.

ARTICLE VI - DILIGENCE

1. **Licensee** shall use its best efforts to bring **Licensed Patent Rights** to market through a thorough, vigorous and diligent program and to continue active, diligent marketing efforts throughout the life of this agreement.

2. **Licensee** shall deliver to **Licensor** on or before _____, a business plan for development of **Licensed Patent Rights**, which includes number and kind of personnel involved, time budgeted and planned for each phase of development and other items as appropriate for the development of the **Licensed Patent Rights**. Quarterly reports describing progress toward meeting the objectives of the business plan shall be provided.

3. **Licensee** shall permit an in-house inspection of **Licensee** facilities by **Licensor** on an annual basis beginning at _____ .

4. **Licensee** failure to perform in accordance with either paragraph 1, 2 or 3.of this ARTICLE VI shall be grounds for **Licensor** to terminate this agreement.

ARTICLE VII - IRREVOCABLE JUDGMENT WITH RESPECT TO VALIDITY OF PATENTS

If a judgment or decree shall be entered in any proceeding in which the validity or infringement of any claim of any patent under which the License is granted hereunder shall be in issue, which judgment or decree shall become not further reviewable though the exhaustion of all permissible applications for rehearing or review by a superior tribunal, or through the expiration of the time permitted for such application, (such a judgment or decree being hereinafter referred to as an irrevocable judgment) the construction placed on any such claim by such irrevocable judgment shall thereafter be followed not only as to such claim, but also as to all claims to which such instruction applies, with respect to acts occurring thereafter and if an irrevocable judgment shall hold any claim invalid, **Licensee** shall be relived thereafter from including in its reports hereunder that portion of the royalties due under ARTICLE III payable only because of such claim or any broader claim to which such irrevocable judgment shall be applicable, and from the performance of any other acts required by this agreement only because of any such claims.

ARTICLE VIII - TERMINATION OR CONVERSION TO NON-EXCLUSIVE LICENSE

1. **Termination by Licensee.**

Option of Licensee: Licensee may terminate the license granted by this agreement, provided **Licensee** shall not be in default hereunder, by giving **Licensor** ninety (90) days notice to its intention to do so. If such notice shall be given, then upon the expiration of such ninety (90) days the termination shall become effective; but such termination shall not operate to relieve **Licensee** from its obligation to pay royalties or to satisfy any other obligations, accrued hereunder prior to the date of such termination.

2. **Termination by Licensor.**

Option of Licensor: Licensor may, at its option, terminate this agreement by written notice to **Licensee** in case of:

a. Default in the payment of any royalties required to be paid by **Licensee** to **Licensor** hereunder

b. Default in the making of any reports required hereunder and such default shall continue for a period of thirty (30) days after **Licensor** shall have given to **Licensee** a written notice of such default.

c. Default in the performance of any other material obligation contained in this agreement on the part of **Licensee** to be performed and such default shall continue for a period of thirty (30) days after **Licensor** shall have given to **Licensee** written notice of such default.

d. Adjudication that **Licensee** is bankrupt or insolvent.

e. The filling by **Licensee** of a petition of bankruptcy, or a petition or answer seeking reorganization, readjustment or rearrangement of its business or affairs under any law or governmental regulation relating to bankruptcy or insolvency.

f. The appointment of a receiver of the business or for all or substantially all of the property of **Licensee**; or the making by **Licensee** of assignment or an attempted assignment for the benefit of its creditors; or the institution by **Licensee** of any proceedings for the liquidation or winding up of its business or affairs.

3   **Effect of termination.**

Termination of this agreement shall not in any way operate to impair or destroy any of **Licensee**'s or **Licensor**'s right or remedies, either at law or in equity, or to relieve **Licensee** of any of its obligations to pay royalties or to comply with any other of the obligations hereunder, accrued prior to the effective date of termination.

4.   **Effect of delay, etc.**

Failure or delay by **Licensor** to exercise its rights of termination hereunder by reason of any default by **Licensee** in carrying out any obligation imposed upon it by this agreement shall not operate to prejudice **Licensor**'s right of termination for any other subsequent default by **Licensee**.

5.   **Option of Licensee to convert to non-exclusive license.**

Licensee shall have the right to convert this License at the same royalty rate as for the exclusive Licensee, without right to sublicense and minimum royalties under **ARTICLE III,** Paragraph 3. shall not be due thereafter.

6.   **Return of Licensed Patent Rights.**

Upon termination of this agreement, all of the **Licensed Patent Rights** shall be returned to **Licensor.** In the event of termination of the agreement by **Licensee** or said conversion of the agreement by **Licensee**, **Licensee** shall grant to **Licensor** a non-exclusive, royalty- free License, with right to sublicense, to manufacture, use and sell improvements including all known-how to **Licensed Patent Rights** made by **Licensee** during the period of this agreement prior to the termination or conversion, to the extent that such improvements are dominated by or derived from the **Licensed Patent Rights**.

ARTICLE IX – TERM

Unless previously terminated as hereinbefore provided, the term of this Agreement shall be from and after the date hereof until the expiration of the last to expire of the licensed issued patents or patents to issue under the **Licensed Patent Rights** under ARTICLE I. **Licensee** shall not be required to pay royalties due only by reason of its use, sale, licensing, lease or sublicensing under issued patents licensed by this Agreement that have expired or been held to be invalid by an Irrevocable Judgment, where there are no other of such issued patents valid and unexpired covering the **Licensee**'s use, sale, licensing, lease or sublicensing; provided, however, that such non-payment of royalties shall not extend to royalty payments already made to **Licensor** more than six (6) months prior to **Licensee**'s discovery of expiration or an Irrevocable Judgment.

ARTICLE X - PATENT LITIGATION

1. **Initiation**. In the event that **Licensor** advises **Licensee** in writing of a substantial infringement of the patents/copyrights included in the **Licensed Patent Rights**, **Licensee** may, but is not obligated

to, bring suit or suits through attorneys of **Licensee**'s selection with respect to such infringement. In the event **Licensee** fails to defend any declaratory judgment action brought against any patent or patents of the **Licensed Patent Rights**, **Licensor** on written notice to **Licensee** may terminate the License as to the particular patent or patents involved in such declaratory judgment action.

2. **Expenses and proceeds of litigation**. Where a suit or suits have been brought by **Licensee, Licensee** shall maintain the litigation at its own expense and shall keep any judgments and awards arising from these suits expecting that portion of the judgments attributable to royalties from the infringer shall be divided equally between **Licensor** and **Licensee** after deducting any and all expenses of such suits; provided, however, **Licensor** shall not be entitled to receive more under this provision than if the infringer had been licensed by **Licensee**.

3. **Licensor's right to sue**. If **Licensee** shall fail to commence suit on an infringement hereunder within one (1) year after the receipt of **Licensor**'s written request to do so. **Licensor** in protection of its reversionary rights shall have the right to bring and prosecute such suits at its cost and expense through attorneys of its selection, in its own name, and all sums received or recovered by **Licensor** in or by reason of such suits shall be retained by **Licensor**; provided, however, no more than one lawsuit at a time shall commence in any such country.

ARTICLE XI - PATENT FILINGS AND PROSECUTING

1. **Licensee** shall pay future costs of the prosecution of the patent applications pending as set forth in ARTICLE I, Paragraph 2. Which are reasonably necessary to obtain a patent. Furthermore, **Licensee** will pay for the costs of filling, prosecuting and maintaining foreign counterpart applications to such pending patent applications, such foreign applications to be filed within ten (10) months prior to the filling date of the corresponding _____ (Country) patent application.

2. **Licensor** shall own improvements by the inventors. **Licensee** shall pay future costs of preparation, filling, prosecuting and maintenance of patents and applications on patentable improvements made by inventors, however, in the event that **Licensee** refuses to file patent applications on such patentable improvements in _____ (Country) and selected foreign countries when requested by **Licensor**, the rights to such patentable improvements for said countries shall be returned to **Licensor**.

3. **Preparation** and maintenance of patent applications and patents undertaken at **Licensee**'s cost shall be performed by patent attorneys selected by **Licensor**; and due diligence and care shall be used in preparing, filling, prosecuting, and maintaining such applications on patentable subject matter. Both parties shall review and approve any and all patent related documents.

4. **Licensee** shall have the right to, on thirty (30) days

written notice to **Licensor**, discontinue payment of its share of the prosecution and/or maintenance costs of any of said patents and/or patent applications. Upon receipt of such written notice, **Licensor** shall have the right to continue such prosecution and/or maintenance on its own name at its own expense in which event the License shall be automatically terminated as to the subject matter claimed in said patents and/or applications.

5. **Notwithstanding** the aforegoing paragraph of this ARTICLE XI, **Licensee**'s obligations under such paragraphs shall continue only so long as **Licensee** continues to have an **Exclusive License** under the **Licensed Patent Rights** and, in the event of conversion of the License to non-exclusive in accordance with ARTICLE VIII, paragraph 1. (b), after the date of such conversion:

    a.   The costs of such thereafter preparation, filing, prosecuting and maintaining of said Licensed patents and patent applications shall be the responsibility of **Licensor**, provided such payments are at the sole discretion of the **Licensor** ; and

    b.   **Licensee** shall have a non-exclusive License without right to sublicense under those of such patents and applications under which **Licensee** had an **Exclusive License** prior to the conversion.

ARTICLE XII - NOTICES, ASSIGNEES

1. **Notices**. Notices and payments required hereunder shall be deemed properly given if duly sent by first

class mail and addressed to the parties at the addresses set forth above. The parties hereto will keep each other advised of address changes.

2. **Assignees, etc.** This Agreement shall be binding upon and shall inure to the benefit of the assigns of **Licensor** and upon and to the benefit of the successors of the entire business of **Licensor**, but neither this agreement nor any of the benefits thereof nor any rights thereunder shall, directly or indirectly, without the prior written consent of **Licensor**, be assigned, divided, or shared by the **Licensor** to or with any other party or parties (except a successor of the entire business of the **Licensor**).

ARTICLE XIII - MISCELLANEOUS

1. **This agreement** is executed and delivered in _____ (Country) and shall be constructed in accordance with the laws of the Government of _____.

2. **No other understanding**. This agreement sets forth the entire agreement and understanding between the parties as to the subject matter thereof and merges all prior discussions between them.

3. **No representations** or warranties regarding patents of third parties. No representations or warranty is made by **Licensor** that the **Licensed Patent Rights** manufactured, used, sold or leased under the **Exclusive License** granted herein is or will be free of claims of infringement of patent rights of any other person or persons. The **Licensor** warrants that it has title to the **Licensed Patent Rights** from

the inventors.

4. **Indemnity.** **Licensee** shall indemnify, hold harmless, and defend **Licensor** and its trustees, officers, employees and agents against any and all allegations and actions for death, illness, personal injury, property damage, and improper business practices arising out of the use of the **Licensed Patent Rights.**

5. **Insurance.** During the term of this agreement, **Licensee** shall, maintain the following insurance coverage:

   a. Commercial general liability with a limit of no less than one million dollars ($1,000,000.00, option) each occurrence. Such insurance shall be written on a standard ISO occurrence form or substitute form providing equivalent coverage.

   b. Professional liability of no less than one million dollars ($1,000,000.00, option) each occurrence.

   c. Workers' compensation consistent with statutory requirements. Certificates of insurance shall be provided to **Licensor** upon request and shall include the provision for 30-day notification to the certificate holder of any cancellation or material alteration in the coverage.

6. **Advertising.** **Licensee** agrees that **Licensee** may not use in any way the name of **Licensor** or any

logotypes or symbols associated with **Licensor** or the names of any researchers without the express written permission of **Licensor**.

7. **Confidentiality**. The parties agree to maintain discussions and proprietary information revealed pursuant to this agreement in confidence, to disclose them only to persons within their respective organizations having a need to know, and to furnish assurances to the other party that such persons understand this duty on confidentiality.

8. **Disclaimer of Warranty**. **Licensed Patent Rights** is experimental in nature and it is provided WITHOUT WARRANTY OR REPRESENTATIONS OF ANY SORT, EXPRESS OR IMPLIED, INCLUDING WITHOUT LIMITATION WARRANTIES OF MERCHANTABILITY AND FITNESS FOR A PARTICULAR PURPOSE OF NON-INFRINGEMENT. **Licensor** makes no representations and provides no warranty that the use of the **Licensed Patent Rights** will not infringe any patent or proprietary rights of third parties.

In witness whereof, the parties hereto have caused this agreement to be executed by their duly authorized representatives.

The effective date of this agreement is _____, 20___.

Licensor _____

Name: _____

Title: _____

Licensee _____

Name:_____

Title: _____

ABOUT THE AUTHOR

*Inventor*preneur multi-millionaire Francisco Guerra is a serial inventor and entrepreneur whose legions of inventions are distributed globally. Particularly known for his inventions in the special effects industry--most especially his snow machine--Francisco's inventions are featured in every major theme park around the world, as well as throughout the film and music video industry. In fact, if you've ever been to Disney World, Universal Studios, Sea World or Busch Gardens, or if you've ever seen *Twilight*, *Harry Potter*, *Elf*, or *The Grinch*, you've probably experienced one of Francisco's inventions for yourself.

Made in the USA
San Bernardino,
CA